Cookie Fun

Cookie Fun

by Judith Hoffman Corwin

A Wanderer Book
Published by Simon & Schuster, Inc.

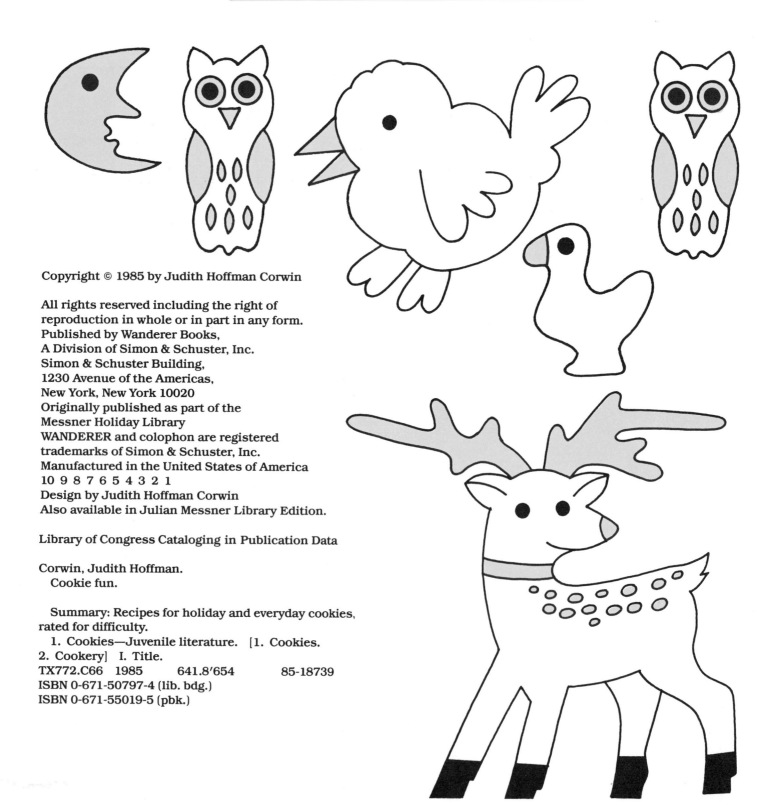

All rights reserved including the right of
reproduction in whole or in part in any form.
Published by Wanderer Books,
A Division of Simon & Schuster, Inc.
Simon & Schuster Building,
1230 Avenue of the Americas,
New York, New York 10020
Originally published as part of the
Messner Holiday Library
WANDERER and colophon are registered
trademarks of Simon & Schuster, Inc.
Manufactured in the United States of America
10 9 8 7 6 5 4 3 2 1
Design by Judith Hoffman Corwin
Also available in Julian Messner Library Edition.

Library of Congress Cataloging in Publication Data

Corwin, Judith Hoffman.
   Cookie fun.

   Summary: Recipes for holiday and everyday cookies,
rated for difficulty.
   1. Cookies—Juvenile literature.   [1. Cookies.
2. Cookery]   I. Title.
TX772.C66   1985   641.8′654   85-18739
ISBN 0-671-50797-4 (lib. bdg.)
ISBN 0-671-55019-5 (pbk.)

For Oliver Jamie, whose very first word was "cookie"

Other books by Judith Hoffman Corwin

Christmas Fun

Easter Fun

Halloween Fun

Patriotic Fun

Thanksgiving Fun

Valentine Fun

Contents

Introduction

Everyone loves cookies! They're fun to make, easy to bake and great to eat. Warm cookies fresh and fragrant from the oven are a special treat to brighten up any day. What could be more pleasing than to bake your very own! Baking cookies is a great way to learn how to measure, stir a batter, judge time, clean up, and share some pleasant conversation with your mom or a friend. Even a younger sister or brother can join in the fun by placing chocolate candies in the center of a cookie. Time shared together in the kitchen will always be remembered.

Even for the beginner there are cookies that are quite simple to make. They don't even need to be baked! Just follow the bear code to decide on the recipe, and create your own treats. The baking tips will also help you to make a perfect batch of cookies on your first try.

Besides those super-simple, no-bake cookies there are five other types of cookies included in **Cookie Fun**. Drop cookies are the easiest because the dough is simply dropped from a spoon onto a cookie sheet. Shaped or molded cookies have the dough shaped into balls with the hands. Rolled cookies are rolled out with the rolling pin on a floured surface, then cut out according to your design. Refrigerator cookies got their name because the dough is shaped into long rolls and chilled in the refrigerator. Then it is sliced and baked. Finally there are bar cookies, for which the dough is placed in a shallow pan and cut into bars or squares after baking.

Old favorites are included, like Chocolate Chocolate Chunk. There are super-nutritious cookies, like Oliver's Outrageous Oatmeal, that taste great and are good for you too! There are also cookies to be tucked into lunch boxes, like Simple Butterscotch, delightful Gingerbread Girl and Boy cookies, and Witch's Brew Cookies. The Handy Cookie or Chocolate Drizzle Cookie are excellent cookies for traveling. These can be mailed to Grandma or to an older sister or brother away at college.

The cookies are grouped by holidays with, lastly, a group of cookies good for any day. The holidays are Christmas, Hanukkah, Valentine's Day, Easter, the Fourth of July, Halloween, Thanksgiving, and birthday. A variety of cookie recipes is given for each holiday, but every holiday section features rolled cookies made from the same cookie recipe but cut to designs and shapes which evoke the spirit of their holiday. See the "basic cookie" recipe on page 16.

Cookie Fun also contains a "recipe bear" which you can use to share your cookie-making "secrets" with your friends.

The pleasures of homemade cookies are many and everyone who mixes up a batch will feel the age-old pride associated with good food and good company.

Bear Code

Each recipe has a bear code. This allows you to judge how much time and effort will be needed to make each kind of cookie.

One-bear recipes are the easiest to make.

Two-bear recipes are easy to make.

Three-bear recipes will take a little more time and patience.

A Few Words for Beginning Bakers

1. Always have an adult's permission to use the kitchen and help to light the oven or stove-top burners.

2. You should always use pot holders when handling any hot saucepans or cookie sheets.

3. An adult should help you put the cookies into the hot oven and remove them.

4. The handles of any saucepans should be turned away from you on the stove so pans won't accidentally be knocked over.

5. If you have trouble rolling out the dough for rolled cookies, chill it for an hour. Then roll out the dough using a pastry cloth. Lightly flour the cloth and the rolling pin. This will stop the dough from sticking. Try and use as little extra flour for this as possible. If you use too much flour it will change the taste of the cookies. Roll the dough from the center out as you lift the rolling pin. Generally the dough should be rolled to a $\frac{1}{4}''$ thickness, or slightly less. If the dough should tear during the rolling, patch it carefully with your fingers, and then continue rolling.

6. When cutting the dough into fancy shapes, like witches and cats, use a dull knife. Be sure to pick up knives by the handle only.

7. Check that the oven is heated to the correct temperature. When baking cookies one batch at a time, place the baking sheet on a rack in the center of the oven. If two batches are to be placed in the oven at the same time, divide the oven into thirds with the racks. Always allow cookie sheets to cool before reusing them or the cookies will spread too much.

8. When a span of cooking time is given, always check the cookies for doneness at the shorter time. When there is one cooking time, check the cookies a minute or two before time is up to avoid overbaking.

9. It's a good idea to remove the baked cookies from the cookie sheets with a metal spatula right after they have been taken from the oven. Put them on wire cooling racks, if you have them, or onto serving platters.

10. Make sure to turn all oven and stove-top dials off when you have finished baking.

About Ingredients

As you read through the recipes in this book you will notice that cookies are made from a few basic ingredients—butter, sugar and flour. With the addition of baking soda or powder, spices and a variety of decorations, many delightful varieties of cookies can be made. Baking is like a chemistry experiment: mix together certain ingredients—and you end up with a cookie!

Most of the recipes use butter, but margarine can be substituted. When measuring the butter, one stick is equal to half a cup, which is usually what is needed. Two sticks equal one cup of butter. When softened butter is needed, take it out of the refrigerator and leave it at room temperature for half an hour or longer before you need to use it.

Three kinds of sugar are used in the recipes—granulated, confectioner's and brown. Often just "sugar" is listed, and then granulated sugar is what is needed. If confectioner's or brown sugar is to be used, the list of ingredients will say so.

All the eggs used are medium size. To separate eggs, if you need to use only the yolks or whites, you will need two bowls. One is for the yolks, the other for the whites. Crack the egg open by hitting it gently in the center against the edge of a bowl. Carefully pull the shell apart and let the white drop into the bowl. Keep the yolk back in one half of the shell. Gently tip the yolk back and forth from one shell half to the other until all of the egg white is separated from the yolk. Then place the yolk in the other bowl.

To beat egg whites use a large bowl because the whites will expand as you beat them. Use an egg beater and make sure that both the bowl and the beater are completely clean and dry. Put the egg whites into the bowl and beat with the egg beater or a wire whisk. Continue to beat until the egg whites form stiff peaks. This will take a few minutes. Be sure to check the bottom of the bowl so that all the egg whites are beaten and become stiff.

Some of the recipes call for baking powder so that the cookies will "rise" or become fluffy and light. The label on the baking powder can should read "double acting" baking powder.

Pre-sifted, all purpose flour is used for all the recipes in this book.

To measure the dry ingredients like the sugar and flour, fill the proper size measuring cup or spoon until it overflows. Do this over the container in which it is stored. Pull a straight edge knife across the top to level off. This leaves a perfectly measured amount.

To measure liquids like orange juice, milk, or water in a measuring cup, pour in the liquid until you reach the desired mark. To measure liquids like vanilla or vegetable oil in a spoon, just pour the liquid into the proper, size measuring spoon until full.

Cooking Utensils

Here is a general list of kitchen utensils used to make the cookies in this book.

mixing bowls: large, medium and small
measuring cups: 1 cup, $\frac{1}{2}$ cup, $\frac{1}{3}$ cup and $\frac{1}{4}$ cup
   size. (or one large measuring cup marked with
   these sizes)
large wooden or plastic mixing spoon
metal or plastic spatula (to remove cookies from
   the cookie sheets)
egg beater
fruit juicer
knife
rolling pin
pastry cloth
pot holders
kitchen timer (or clock or watch)
cookie sheets
wire racks (for cookies to cool on)
9-inch square baking pan
tinfoil, waxed paper
airtight containers
toothpicks (to insert into cookies to test for doneness)

Needed for cleanup:

paper towels or dishcloth
dishwashing liquid
sponges

Starting to Bake

Whether you are a beginning baker or have had some experience in the kitchen, these suggestions will help you to make the delicious cookies in this book.

1. Be sure to read through each recipe from start to finish before beginning to bake.

2. Check that you have everything you need to make the cookies. If not, make a shopping list and ask someone to buy the needed ingredients.

3. Always wash your hands before you handle any food or begin cooking.

4. Clear a working space in the kitchen so you can have enough room to work in.

5. Collect all the cooking equipment that you will need before you actually begin to bake.

6. Follow the recipes exactly as they are written. Later on, if you like, you can experiment and make your own variations.

7. Since cookies bake in a very short time (usually 10–12 minutes), use a kitchen timer or be sure to check the time on a clock every time you put a batch of cookies into the oven. They burn quickly if left too long inside, so you must keep track of the time.

8. When you have finished baking, wash the dishes that you have used and clean up the kitchen. Put everything away as you found it when you began. The next person to use the kitchen will really appreciate this and will then be happy to allow you to bake more cookies. It might be easier to clean up as you go along and rinse the bowls and spoons as you use them. Placing them to soak in a sink full of water makes them easier to wash if you want to wait until after your cookies are done.

9. Invite your family and friends for cookies and milk to sample your creative productions!

10. Leftover cookies—if there are any!—should be stored in airtight containers. Crisp cookies can be stored directly in the containers. Soft cookies and frosted ones should be placed between layers of waxed paper. This will keep them from sticking together.

Have fun and enjoy the many delicious cookies that there are to be made!

The "Basic Cookie" Recipe

Use this recipe to make rolled cookies for each of the holidays. As you will see different designs and shapes are suggested for each holiday, and patterns are given for them at the beginning of each holiday section. The designs and shapes can all be cut out from the same dough. The directions under each holiday, for this type of rolled cookie, will therefore refer you to the "basic cookie" recipe given below.

INGREDIENTS YOU WILL NEED TO MAKE THE
   COOKIES:

1 cup sweet butter, softened
8 ounce package cream cheese
¾ cup sugar
2 teaspoons vanilla
3½ cups all-purpose flour
extra flour to roll out the dough
extra vegetable shortening to grease the cookie
   sheets

MATERIALS YOU WILL NEED FOR PATTERNS:

tracing paper   pencil
oaktag   scissors

UTENSILS YOU WILL NEED:

measuring cups and spoons
large mixing bowl
wooden spoon, spatula, cookie sheets
pot holders, to remove cookie sheets from the
   oven
toothpicks (to apply the icing to the cookies)
paper towels, 5 small bowls or cups

DIRECTIONS:

1. Stir the butter in the large mixing bowl until it is light and fluffy. Beat in the cream cheese, a little at a time.

2. Now add the sugar and vanilla. Add the flour and continue to stir the mixture until it is completely combined. You will now have a nice stiff dough to work with.

3. Roll the dough into ¼″ thickness on a lightly floured surface.

4. Preheat the oven to 350°. Ask an adult to help you with this.

5. Trace the patterns for all the designs on the tracing paper. Now put the tracing paper on top of the oaktag and hold together with one hand. With the other hand, cut all around the outside edge. Repeat this for all of the designs until you have an oaktag pattern for each of them.

6. Place the cardboard pattern on the rolled-out dough. Again hold it in place with one hand and cut all around the outside edge with a knife. Lift the pattern and repeat for all of the designs. Make as many cookies of each design as you like.

16

7. After the cookies have been cut out with the patterns, place them one inch apart on lightly greased cookie sheets.

8. Bake for 10-15 minutes, or until lightly browned. Allow to cool.

9. Ice with either the chocolate icing, colored icing or prepared icing that comes in tubes. The prepared icing can be bought in the supermarket in a variety of colors. Another super-simple way of decorating these cookies is to spread sifted confectioners' sugar over them. Just put the cooled cookies onto a large sheet of waxed paper and sift a little of the sugar over each cookie to give it a gentle "dusting."

Note: Eyes can be made with either raisins or small candies. This is if you aren't going to "paint" them on with the colored icing. Chocolate sprinkles, colored sugars, chopped nuts, silver dragees, cinnamon red-hots or small chocolate covered candies can also be used to decorate the cookies. These should be put onto the cookies before they are baked.

Colored Icing

INGREDIENTS:

2 egg whites
½ teaspoon cream of tartar
3 cups sifted confectioners' sugar
red, yellow, blue and green food coloring

DIRECTIONS:

1. In a medium bowl, beat the egg whites (with the egg beater) and the cream of tartar until very foamy.

2. Beat in the confectioners' sugar gradually, until the icing stands in firm peaks and is stiff enough to hold a sharp line when cut through with a knife.

3. Divide the icing among five small bowls; leave one plain (white); tint the remaining with food coloring. Using a toothpick ice the cookies. To keep the icing from drying out while you are working with it, cover the bowls with damp paper toweling. Store any leftover icing in tightly covered jars in the refrigerator. Makes about 1¼ cups of icing.

Chocolate Icing

INGREDIENTS:

2 cups sifted confectioners' sugar
½ cup unsweetened cocoa powder
4 tablespoons milk
2 teaspoons vanilla
2 tablespoons butter, softened

DIRECTIONS:

1. In a medium bowl, blend together the sugar and cocoa. Add the milk and vanilla. Stir until smooth.

2. Add the butter and continue to stir until mixture is completely combined. If necessary, add a drop or two of additional milk or a teaspoon of sugar to give the icing a good spreading consistency. Cover and set aside until needed.

3. Spoon the icing over the warm cookies and allow them to cool until the icing has set. This may take several hours. This makes about 1 cup of icing.

18

Recipe Bears

These bears are really easy to make and add a thoughtful touch when you want to give some cookies to a friend.

MATERIALS:

8 ½″ × 11″ piece of white paper
tracing paper
pencil
scissors
colored felt tip markers

METHOD:

1. One piece of paper makes one recipe bear.

2. Trace the pattern for the bear onto the tracing paper.

3. Place the pattern on the paper and hold together with one hand. With the other, cut along the outline. Unfold the paper and you have your bear.

4. With the felt tip markers draw in the bear's face, paws and bow, as shown.

5. On the reverse side write carefully and neatly the recipe that you chose to give to a friend.

6. To prepare the cookies that you are giving to a friend, wrap them in a piece of tinfoil. Then place the tinfoil bundle in a plastic bag. Be sure to close the plastic bag with a rubber band to keep the air out. Usually a dozen or so cookies makes a nice amount to give away.

7. The recipe bear can be attached to the plastic bag with a clear piece of tape. Or you could make a small hole in one of its ears and put a piece of yarn through it. Tie the yarn around the rubber band.

You might want to give cookies away in a more decorative container. A great one might be a wicker or raffia basket that you have permission to give away. Put the plastic bag into the basket and tie a ribbon on. Attach the recipe bear as before.

An empty shoe box also makes a nice container for cookies. Again the cookies must first be wrapped in tinfoil and then placed in a plastic bag. This will keep them fresher longer. You can make paper flowers and glue them onto the box to decorate it. Attach a recipe bear as before.

A clean glass jar with a tight-fitting lid is still another idea for a container for cookies. If you use a glass jar you can simply put the cookies right into the jar without wrapping them in tinfoil or plastic.

All of these are fun ways to share your delicious cookies with a friend, a special treat made even better by the recipe bear. He carries the recipe so your friend will also be able to make his own cookies!

Christmas Cookies

For a special Christmas treat make these rolled cookies in the shape of a Santa, candy cane, star, reindeer, angel and Christmas tree. The designs are given below; instructions for using the designs and baking the cookies are given on page 16.

Snowmen Cookies

Now you will be able to make snowmen whenever you want, even in the summer. They melt in your mouth!

INGREDIENTS:

1 cup butter, softened
¼ cup confectioner's sugar
1 teaspoon almond extract
2 cups flour
1 cup finely chopped almonds
extra confectioner's sugar to sift over the cookies
raisins for snowmen's eyes
small red candies for snowmen's buttons
toothpicks for snowmen's arms

DIRECTIONS:

1. Stir the butter, confectioner's sugar and almond extract together until completely blended.

2. Add the flour gradually to the mixture and then the almonds. Beat well.

3. Divide the dough in half and wrap each half in a piece of waxed paper. Place the wrapped dough in the refrigerator for an hour to allow it to become firm enough to shape into balls.

4. Preheat the oven to 350°.

5. Remove one portion of dough from the refrigerator. For easier handling of the dough, make one snowman at a time. Checking the illustration, shape a small amount of dough in the palm of your hand into three balls of different sizes. Carefully press the three balls together to make a snowman. Do this step right on an ungreased cookie sheet. After finishing one snowman make another, leaving about two inches between them. Repeat until all this dough and the remaining dough from the refrigerator has been used up.

6. Again checking the illustration, place the raisin eyes and candy buttons on each snowman before putting them in the oven. Bake for 15–18 minutes or until very slightly browned.

7. With a spatula, gently remove the cookies from the cookie sheets and allow to cool for five minutes.

8. Put the extra confectioner's sugar into a sifter and sift over the snowmen. Expect some of the extra sugar to melt into the cookies. With your fingers, brush the sugar off the eyes and buttons so that you are able to see them on the finished cookie.

9. To make each snowman's arms, you will need four toothpicks. Push two toothpicks into each side of the snowman's middle. Look at the illustration for proper placement.

10. Depending on the size of the snowmen that you make, this recipe should make about two dozen.

Stained Glass Cookies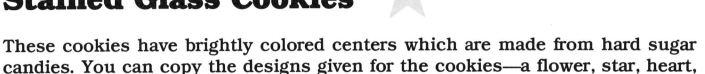

These cookies have brightly colored centers which are made from hard sugar candies. You can copy the designs given for the cookies—a flower, star, heart, clover and diamond.

INGREDIENTS:

$\frac{1}{2}$ cup butter
6 tablespoons sugar
1 egg, beaten
$\frac{1}{2}$ teaspoon vanilla
$1\frac{1}{4}$ cups flour
$\frac{1}{2}$ teaspoon baking powder

$\frac{1}{2}$ teaspoon salt
extra flour to roll out the dough
hard sugar candy in flavors like cinnamon, wild cherry, lemon, orange, tangerine, lime and butterscotch.

DIRECTIONS:

1. Prepare cookie sheets by lining them with a sheet of tinfoil.

2. Combine the butter and sugar. Add the egg and vanilla. Continue stirring until mixture is completely blended.

3. Add the flour, baking powder, and salt. Stir well. You will now have a stiff dough. Wrap the dough in wax paper and chill for one hour.

4. Roll the dough to a $\frac{1}{4}''$ thickness on a lightly floured surface.

5. These cookies will be made into very simple shapes so you won't have to make a pattern. Just look at the illustrations and then with a dull knife cut out the designs that you would like to make. Make each cookie about three inches in size. After you have cut out each cookie, cut out an inch square in the center of each. This is where the candy will go.

6. Separate the candy into each of the colors you will be using. Break it into small pieces by placing it between two sheets of tinfoil and hit-ting gently with a wooden spoon.

7. Heat the oven to 350°.

8. Place the cookies on the tinfoil-covered cookie sheets with a metal spatula. Fill each hole with candy until it is level with the dough.

9. Bake for about 10 minutes or until cookies are lightly browned along the edges. The candy should be melted. If the cookies are ready, but the candy has not completely melted, remove them from the oven anyway. Gently spread the candy around the hole with a knife. Allow to cool and then carefully remove the cookies from the cookie sheets. Makes about three dozen cookies.

24

Gingerbread Girl and Boy Cookies

Everyone loves these charming gingerbread cookies and they have been a long-time tradition at holidays. In fourteenth-century Europe they were baked and sold at carnivals. Later at holiday time in the Scandinavian countries they were baked and beautifully decorated with white sugar icing. The early American settlers even brought their recipes for gingerbread cookies with them to be enjoyed in their new home.

INGREDIENTS:

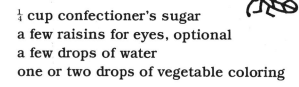

1½ sticks butter, softened
½ cup sugar
1 egg yolk
2½ tablespoons corn syrup
2 cups flour
1 teaspoon baking soda
¼ teaspoon salt
1 teaspoon cinnamon
2 teaspoons ground ginger
extra flour to roll out the dough
extra butter to grease the cookie sheets

¼ cup confectioner's sugar
a few raisins for eyes, optional
a few drops of water
one or two drops of vegetable coloring

MATERIALS NEEDED FOR PATTERNS:

tracing paper
oaktag
pencil
scissors

DIRECTIONS:

1. Combine the butter and sugar. Add the egg yolk and corn syrup. Continue stirring until mixture is completely blended.

2. Add the flour, baking soda, salt, cinnamon and ginger. Stir well. You will now have a stiff dough. Wrap the dough in wax paper and chill for several hours. If you do not want to use all the dough at once, you can leave some in the refrigerator for another day.

3. Roll the dough to ¼″ thickness on a lightly floured surface. Use the pattern on the opposite page to make your gingerbread girl and boy.

4. Trace the pattern on the tracing paper. Now put the tracing paper pattern on top of a piece of the oaktag and hold together with one hand. With the other hand cut all around the outside edge.

5. Place the cardboard pattern on the rolled-out dough. Hold it in place again with one hand, and cut all around the outside edge with a knife. Lift the pattern and repeat.

6. Preheat the oven to 350°.

7. After the cookies have been cut out, place them one inch apart on a lightly greased cookie sheet. You can use raisins to make the eyes for the gingerbread girls and boys or use the icing to "paint" them on. Bake for about 15 minutes.

8. The patterns that are given for the ginger-bread girl and boy have been decorated with icing. You can also use icing to create the eyes, mouth, hair and clothes. To make the icing, combine $\frac{1}{4}$ cup confectioner's sugar and a few drops of water. Decide how many colors you are going to make and put a small amount of this mixture into separate bowls. Then add a drop or

two of vegetable coloring. Mix well. Apply the icing with a cotton swab that has been dipped in water and squeezed out smooth. You can also use a small knife to apply the icing. There are also ready-made icings that can be bought in a supermarket. They come in tubes in several different colors and have small tips that may be used like a pencil to color in your gingerbread cookies.

Hanukkah Cookies

For a special Hanukkah treat make these rolled cookies in the shape of a dreidel, candle and six-pointed star. The designs are given below; instructions for using the designs and baking the cookies are given on page 16.

Half-moon Cookies

Half-moon shaped cookies dating back to the seventeenth century are special Hanukkah melt-in-your-mouth treats.

INGREDIENTS:

1 cup butter, softened
¼ cup confectioners' sugar
2 cups flour
⅓ cup ground almonds
extra flour used to shape the cookies
extra confectioners' sugar to sift over the cookies

DIRECTIONS:

1. Preheat the oven to 350°.

2. Combine the butter and sugar. Add the flour and continue stirring until mixture is completely blended.

3. Add the ground almonds and mix well.

4. Now you are ready to shape the dough into half-moon cookies. Sprinkle some extra flour onto your working surface and begin by taking a handful of dough at a time. Roll the dough into a long one-inch wide cylinder. Now cut the cylinder into one-and-a-half-inch lengths. Make these into small half-moon shapes. Place them on ungreased cookie sheets. Repeat this until all the dough has been used up.

5. Bake for 10-15 minutes, or until lightly browned. Remove the cookies to wire racks to cool. Put the extra confectioners's sugar into a sifter and lightly dust the cooled cookies. Makes about two dozen cookies.

Valentine's Day Cookies

For a special Valentine's Day treat make these rolled cookies in the shape of a heart, dove, cupid and butterfly. The designs are given below; instructions for using the designs and baking the cookies are given on page 16.

Peanut Butter Chocolate Kiss Cookies

A chocolate kiss candy is placed in the center of each of these cookies for an extra treat.

INGREDIENTS:

$\frac{3}{4}$ cup butter
$\frac{3}{4}$ cup chunky peanut butter
1 cup sugar
1 egg
$\frac{1}{2}$ cup milk
3 cups flour
14 oz. package of chocolate kisses candies

DIRECTIONS:

1. Set oven at 350°.

2. Stir the butter and peanut butter together until well mixed.

3. Add the sugar and the egg and mix.

4. Add the flour and the milk. Mix well.

5. Take a small amount of dough out of the mixing bowl and roll between your palms into a ball about the size of a big marble. Place the balls as you make them on the cookie sheet about two inches apart. When all the dough is used up, take a chocolate kiss and push it into the center of each cookie.

6. Place the cookie sheets in the oven for 10–12 minutes. Makes four dozen cookies.

Chocolate Drizzle Cookies

These cookies have sour cream and cinnamon in them and chocolate frosting drizzled over them.

INGREDIENTS:

2 cups flour
1 teaspoon baking powder
$\frac{1}{2}$ teaspoon baking soda
$\frac{1}{2}$ teaspoon salt
1 teaspoon cinnamon
$\frac{1}{2}$ cup butter, softened
1 cup light brown sugar
1 egg
2 teaspoons vanilla
$\frac{1}{2}$ cup sour cream
extra butter to grease the cookie sheets
6 ounces semisweet chocolate
1 tablespoon vegetable oil

DIRECTIONS:

1. Preheat the oven to 350°.

2. Combine the flour, baking powder, baking soda, salt and cinnamon. Stir well.

3. Add the butter and sugar. Continue stirring until light and fluffy. Beat in the egg and vanilla.

4. Slowly add the sour cream until the mixture is completely combined.

5. Using the extra butter, grease the cookie sheets.

6. Drop rounded tablespoons of batter onto the cookie sheets about two inches apart. Place in the oven and bake for 10–12 minutes or until lightly browned.

7. Allow the cookies to cool. Meanwhile, melt the chocolate in a small saucepan over medium heat. Add the vegetable oil and stir until completely combined.

8. Take a teaspoon of the melted chocolate at a time and drizzle it over each cookie. Repeat until all the cookies have chocolate on them. Makes about four dozen cookies.

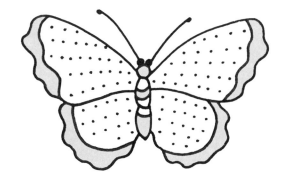

Easter Cookies

For a special Easter treat make these rolled cookies in the shape of a bunny, duck and chick. The designs are given below; instructions for using the designs and baking the cookies are given on page 16.

Creative Critter Cookies

There are cookie illustrations for a raccoon, horse, dog, cat, panda, fish, bumblebee and a squirrel. Cut, shape and squeeze the chocolate and vanilla dough to form these cute critters.

INGREDIENTS FOR CHOCOLATE DOUGH:

$\frac{1}{2}$ cup butter
$\frac{1}{2}$ cup sugar
1 egg yolk
1 teaspoon vanilla
$1\frac{1}{4}$ cups flour
6 tablespoons cocoa
2 tablespoons vegetable oil

INGREDIENTS FOR VANILLA DOUGH:

$\frac{1}{2}$ cup butter
$\frac{1}{2}$ cup sugar
1 egg yolk
$\frac{1}{2}$ teaspoon vanilla
$1\frac{1}{4}$ cups flour

DIRECTIONS:

1. To make the chocolate dough, combine the butter and sugar. Add the egg yolk and continue stirring until mixture is completely blended.

2. Add the vanilla, flour, cocoa and vegetable oil. Stir well. To make the vanilla dough, follow steps 1 and 2, omitting the cocoa and vegetable oil.

3. Choose which one of the cookie creatures you would like to make: a raccoon, horse, dog, cat, panda, fish, bumblebee or squirrel. The illustrations will give you an idea of what you can do with this chocolate and vanilla dough. You can cut and shape the dough without making a pattern. Alternate the chocolate and vanilla to give your animal cookies beautiful detail. If you like, you can make up your own critters.

4. Form the animals on ungreased cookie sheets. Preheat the oven to 350°. Roll out the chocolate and vanilla dough separately to $\frac{1}{4}''$ thickness. Break off small pieces to begin making your animals. You can also cut the dough into shapes with a dull knife to build your critters. Then you can begin to shape and squeeze the dough, almost as if you were sculpting it out of clay.

5. Bake for about 10 minutes or until lightly browned. Allow to cool. Makes about two dozen cookies, depending on the size of the critters you make.

The Fourth of July Cookies

For a special Fourth of July treat make these rolled cookies in the shape of an eagle, flag, donkey and elephant. The designs are given below; instructions for using the designs and baking the cookies are given on page 16.

Rainbow Cookies

These red, white, and blue delights are fun to make and beautiful to serve.

INGREDIENTS:

$\frac{1}{2}$ cup butter
$1\frac{1}{2}$ cups confectioner's sugar
1 egg, beaten
1 teaspoon almond extract
$2\frac{1}{4}$ cups flour
1 teaspoon baking soda
$\frac{1}{2}$ teaspoon salt
red and blue vegetable coloring
24 maraschino cherry halves

DIRECTIONS:

1. Stir the butter and sugar together until well mixed.

2. Add the egg and the almond extract.

3. Add the flour, baking soda, and salt. Mix well.

4. Divide the dough into three equal parts. Now add one or two drops of red vegetable coloring to one portion of the dough and mix well. Repeat with the blue vegetable coloring to the second portion of dough and leave the remaining portion of dough white.

5. Wrap each portion of dough separately in waxed paper and allow to chill in the refrigerator for at least one hour.

6. Preheat the oven to 350°.

7. Starting with one of the colors of chilled dough, take a small amount and roll it between your palms into a ball about the size of a big marble. Place the balls as you make them on ungreased cookie sheets about two inches apart.

8. Place the maraschino cherry halves on a paper towel to drain. Before putting the cookies into the oven, gently push a cherry half into the center of each cookie.

9. Bake for 12–15 minutes. Watch the cookies carefully as they are baking so that they keep their beautiful color and don't burn along the edges. Makes about four dozen cookies.

40

Bravo Brownies

Whenever you make these brownies they will quickly disappear and your friends will say, "Bravo! More please!"

INGREDIENTS:

½ cup vegetable oil
6 tablespoons unsweetened cocoa
1 egg, beaten
1 cup sugar
1¼ cups flour
½ teaspoon salt
½ teaspoon baking soda
1 teaspoon vanilla
¾ cup orange juice
1 cup semisweet chocolate pieces
extra vegetable oil to grease the 9″ × 9″ × 2″ baking pan

DIRECTIONS:

1. Grease the baking pan and then preheat the oven to 350°.

2. In a large mixing bowl combine the vegetable oil, cocoa, egg, sugar, flour, salt, baking soda, vanilla, and orange juice. Beat until smooth and fully blended.

3. Add the semisweet chocolate pieces and stir well.

4. Spread the batter evenly in the greased baking pan with a spatula.

5. Bake for 30 minutes or until a toothpick inserted into the center of the brownies comes out clean. Allow to cool in the pan and then cut into 3-inch squares. Makes nine large, moist, and chewy brownies. Bravo!

Halloween Cookies

For a special Halloween treat make these rolled cookies in the shape of a pumpkin, ghost and bat. The designs are given below; instructions for using the designs and baking the cookies are given on page 16.

Pumpkin Butter Cookies

These cookies are easily made into a small pumpkin shape. The center of each can be filled with jam, a walnut piece or a chocolate candy.

INGREDIENTS:

½ cup butter, softened
¼ cup sugar
1 egg yolk
1 cup flour (heaping)
strawberry jam, or walnuts or small chocolate
    candies

DIRECTIONS:

1. Cream the butter and the sugar together.

2. Stir in the egg yolk and then gradually add the flour.

3. Form into a ball. Wrap in wax paper. Refrigerate for half an hour.

4. Preheat the oven to 350°.

5. To make the cookies, take a little bit of the dough into your hand and roll into a small ball. Pinch the top edge slightly and draw out a small piece to make the pumpkin's stem. Make a hole in the center of each cookie with your finger, and fill with jam, a walnut piece or a chocolate candy.

6. Place the cookies on cookie sheets and bake for about 20–25 minutes or until slightly browned. Makes about two dozen cookies.

Witch's Brew Cookies

Brew up a batch of Wendy Witch's butter cookies in a very short time, and entertain your friends. There are patterns to make Wendy herself, her trusty cat, a toad, snake, lizard, lightning bolt, moon and star. Arrange them on a platter with a paper doily underneath and you are ready to have a party.

INGREDIENTS:

½ cup vegetable shortening
½ cup sugar
½ cup honey
1 egg yolk
1 teaspoon vanilla
1½ cups flour
1 teaspoon baking soda
extra flour to roll out the dough
extra vegetable shortening to grease the cookie sheets
a few raisins for eyes, optional
2 cups confectioner's sugar
¼ cup butter
3 or 4 tablespoons orange juice
prepared icing (it comes in small tubes)

MATERIALS NEEDED FOR PATTERNS:

tracing paper
oaktag
pencil
scissors

DIRECTIONS:

1. Combine the vegetable shortening, sugar and honey. Add the egg yolk and continue stirring until mixture is completely blended.

2. Now add the vanilla, flour and baking soda. Stir well.

3. Roll the dough to ¼″ thickness on a lightly floured surface. Use the patterns given to make your witch, cat, toad, snake, lizard, moon, star and lightning bolt.

4. Trace the patterns for all the designs on the tracing paper. Now put the tracing paper on top of the oaktag and hold together with one hand. With the other hand, cut all around the outside edge. Repeat this for all of the designs until you have an oaktag pattern for each.

5. Place the cardboard pattern on the rolled-out dough. Hold it in place again with one hand and cut all around the outside edge with a knife. Lift the pattern and repeat for all of the designs. Make as many cookies of each design as you like.

6. Heat the oven to 350°.

7. After the cookies have been cut out with the

44

patterns, place them one inch apart on lightly greased cookie sheets. You can use raisins for eyes.

8.   Bake for 10 minutes, or until lightly browned. Allow to cool. Makes about two dozen cookies.

9.   For an extra touch, if you like, you can spread the following icing over the cooled cookies. Combine two cups of confectioner's sugar with $\frac{1}{4}$ cup of soft butter. Beat in three or four table-spoons of orange juice until you have a smooth icing that is easily spreadable. With a knife carefully spread the icing over the cookies. Makes one cup of icing. If you prefer, you can use prepared icing. The instructions are printed on the tube.

These cookies might be fun to serve with cranberry juice or a mixture of one part apple juice with one part pineapple juice.

45

Thanksgiving Cookies

For a special Thanksgiving treat make these rolled cookies in the shape of a turkey and leaf. The designs are given below; instructions for using the designs and baking the cookies are given on page 16.

48

Peanut Butter Butterscotch Cookies

These crunchy cookies taste great, are super-fast to make and don't even have to be baked!

INGREDIENTS:

$\frac{1}{2}$ cup creamy peanut butter
two 6-ounce packages butterscotch pieces
6 cups cornflakes

DIRECTIONS:

1. In a large saucepan combine the peanut butter and butterscotch pieces. Put the saucepan on the stove over medium heat. Continue to stir the mixture until it is completely melted and combined.

2. Remove the saucepan from the heat and stir in the cornflakes. Stir well.

3. Put waxed paper onto cookie sheets. Then drop the batter from a teaspoon onto the waxed paper. Refrigerate for half an hour to allow the cookies to set. Serve. Makes about three dozen cookies.

Spice Cookies

"Sugar and spice"—in this case cinnamon, cloves and nutmeg—combine to give these cookies their zest.

INGREDIENTS:

1 cup butter
2 cups brown sugar
2 eggs, beaten
$\frac{1}{4}$ cup orange juice
3 cups flour
1 teaspoon baking soda
$\frac{1}{2}$ teaspoon salt
2 teaspoons cinnamon
1 teaspoon nutmeg
1 teaspoon ground cloves
$\frac{1}{2}$ cup seedless raisins
$\frac{1}{2}$ cup chopped walnuts, optional
extra butter to grease the cookie sheets

DIRECTIONS:

1. Preheat the oven to 375°.

2. Stir the butter and brown sugar together until well mixed.

3. Continue to mix and add the eggs and the orange juice.

4. Add the flour, baking soda and salt and stir into the batter.

5. Now add the spices—cinnamon, nutmeg and cloves—to the batter. Beat well.

6. Add the raisins and the walnuts, if you wish, and mix in until blended.

7. Grease the cookie sheets with the extra butter.

8. Drop about a tablespoon of dough for each cookie onto the cookie sheets. These cookies spread while they are baking so be sure to leave them about three inches apart.

9. Bake for 12–15 minutes. Makes about three dozen cookies.

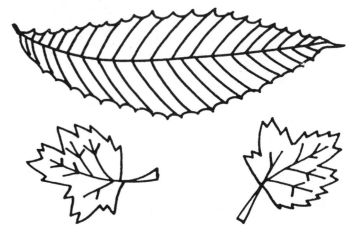

Shorty Shortbread Cookies

These Scotch shortbread cookies can be cut into fancy shapes if you like or simply rolled out and cut into squares.

INGREDIENTS:

¾ cup sugar
1½ cups butter, softened
4 cups flour
extra flour to roll dough out with

DIRECTIONS:

1. Preheat the oven to 350°.

2. Stir the butter and sugar together thoroughly. Add one cup of flour at a time to the mixture. Mix well.

3. Dust the counter that you are going to roll your dough out on with the extra flour. Roll the dough to a $\frac{1}{4}''$ thickness. Cut into squares or use a fancy cookie cutter.

4. Place cookies on ungreased cookie sheets, an inch apart.

5. Bake for 20 minutes or until light brown in color. Makes about three dozen cookies.

Birthday Cookies

For a special birthday treat make these rolled "age" and "me" cookies. Designs are given below for numbers and for a girl and boy. Instructions for using the designs and baking the cookies are given on page 16.

For your special birthday "me" cookies, be sure to write your name on them with icing.

1 2 3 4

5 6 7 8

9 10

The Handy Cookie

Here's a fun way to make your own hand into a cookie and also to send a special birthday message to a friend.

INGREDIENTS:

$\frac{1}{2}$ cup butter, softened
1 cup sugar
1 egg
$\frac{1}{2}$ teaspoon vanilla
2 tablespoons lemon juice

$\frac{1}{4}$ cup orange juice
$1\frac{1}{2}$ teaspoons baking powder
2 cups flour
extra flour to roll out dough
extra butter to grease the cookie sheets

DIRECTIONS:

1. Preheat the oven to 350°.

2. Stir the butter and sugar together until well mixed.

3. Add the egg and the vanilla. Now add the lemon juice and the orange juice. Beat until the mixture is light and fluffy.

4. Add the baking powder and flour to the mixture. Stir until completely combined.

5. Wrap the dough in waxed paper and allow to chill in the refrigerator for one hour.

6. Lightly sprinkle some of the extra flour onto the surface that you are going to use to roll out your dough.

7. Divide the dough in half and put one half back into the refrigerator until you are ready to use it. Roll out the remaining dough to $\frac{1}{4}''$ thickness.

8. Place your hand on the rolled-out dough and carefully cut around the outline with a dull knife. You will need an adult to help supervise this part.

9. Carefully lift up the cookie with a spatula and place it on a cookie sheet that has been greased with some of the extra butter. Leave about an inch of space between cookies. After you have used up the first half of the dough, roll out the remaining dough and then repeat steps 8 and 9.

10. Bake for 12–15 minutes or until lightly browned.

11. With a felt-tip marker write your birthday message on a small piece of paper (about 2″ square). Make a border around the message with small designs to make it even more special.

12. To make the "glue" to attach the message to the cookie, make a paste by adding a few drops of water to a teaspoon of sugar.

13. Use your finger to put a little "glue" onto the reverse side of each corner of the paper. Place the message on the cookie. Now you are ready to exchange cookie hand messages with your friends. Makes about two dozen cookies.

Chocolate Chilled Cookies

A great treat to send to a friend as a special gift.

INGREDIENTS:

$1\frac{1}{4}$ cups butter
$1\frac{1}{4}$ cups sugar
2 teaspoons vanilla extract
1 egg, beaten
4 ounces (squares) unsweetened baker's chocolate
3 cups flour
1 teaspoon baking powder
$\frac{1}{2}$ teaspoon salt
$\frac{1}{3}$ cup orange juice
extra sugar to sprinkle onto cookies before baking

DIRECTIONS:

1. Stir the butter and sugar together until well mixed.

2. Add the egg and vanilla extract.

3. Melt the chocolate in a small saucepan over medium heat. Add the melted chocolate to the mixture and blend thoroughly.

4. Add the flour, baking powder and salt. Now pour the orange juice into the mixture and stir until completely blended in.

5. Place the dough on a large piece of waxed paper and shape into a roll 2″ in diameter. Wrap the waxed paper around the roll of dough and allow to chill overnight in the refrigerator.

6. Next day, preheat the oven to 350°.

7. Cut the dough in $\frac{1}{8}''$ slices.

8. Place the cookies on ungreased cookie sheets about an inch apart. Sprinkle some sugar onto each cookie before baking.

9. Bake for 10 minutes. Makes about fifty cookies.

55

Any Day Cookies

Rolled cookies for an any day treat can be made from the designs given below for a teddy bear, owl, cat, house, turtle and lion. Instructions for using the designs and baking the cookies are given on page 16.

Oliver's Outrageous Oatmeal Cookies

Oatmeal cookies are a popular standby in our house and a special favorite of Oliver's.

INGREDIENTS:

$\frac{1}{2}$ cup butter
1 cup light brown sugar
1 egg, beaten
1 teaspoon vanilla
$\frac{3}{4}$ cup flour
$\frac{1}{2}$ teaspoon salt
$\frac{1}{2}$ teaspoon baking powder
$1\frac{1}{2}$ cups instant oatmeal
$\frac{1}{4}$ cup raisins
$\frac{1}{2}$ cup semisweet chocolate pieces
$\frac{1}{4}$ cup chopped coconut
$\frac{1}{4}$ cup chopped walnuts, optional

DIRECTIONS:

1. Preheat the oven to 350°.

2. Stir the butter, brown sugar and egg together. Add the vanilla and beat well.

3. Add the flour, salt, and baking powder. Mix well.

4. Stir in the instant oatmeal until completely combined.

5. Add the raisins, chocolate pieces and coconut to the batter. If you like you can also add the walnuts. Mix well.

6. Drop from a teaspoon onto ungreased cookie sheets.

7. Bake for 10 minutes. Makes about fifty cookies.

Wonder Chocolate Cookies

These wonderful cookies don't even have to be baked, so they are a perfect first-time cookie to make.

INGREDIENTS:

½ cup butter
½ cup milk
½ cup chocolate syrup
2 cups sugar
½ teaspoon salt
3 cups quick-cooking rolled oats
1 teaspoon vanilla
1 cup flaked coconut
½ cup chopped walnuts, optional

DIRECTIONS:

1. In a large saucepan combine the butter, milk, chocolate syrup, sugar and salt. Put the saucepan on the stove over medium heat and stir until the mixture is completely combined. Bring to a boil and then remove from the heat.

2. Add the rolled oats, vanilla, coconut and chopped walnuts (if desired).

3. Put waxed paper onto cookie sheets. Then drop the batter from a teaspoon onto the waxed paper. Refrigerate for half an hour to allow cookies to set. Serve. Makes about four dozen cookies.

Chocolate Chocolate Chunk Cookies

These perfect chocolate cookies are made even better by adding small chunks of chocolate to them.

INGREDIENTS:

$\frac{1}{2}$ cup butter
$\frac{3}{4}$ cup light brown sugar
1 egg, beaten
1 teaspoon vanilla
$\frac{1}{2}$ teaspoon baking soda
1 tablespoon orange juice
$1\frac{3}{4}$ cups flour
4 tablespoons powdered cocoa
$\frac{1}{2}$ lb. semisweet chocolate cut into small chunks

DIRECTIONS:

1. Preheat the oven to 350°.

2. Stir the butter, sugar and egg together. Add the vanilla and beat well.

3. Add the baking soda and orange juice to the mixture. Beat well.

4. Stir in the flour and the powdered cocoa; add the small chocolate chunks and mix well.

5. Drop from a teaspoon onto ungreased cookie sheets.

6. Bake for 12–15 minutes. Makes about four dozen cookies.

Simple Butterscotch Cookies

Butterscotch cookies are great to eat and great to bake.

INGREDIENTS:

1 cup butter
2 cups dark brown sugar
2 eggs, beaten
$\frac{1}{2}$ teaspoon baking soda
$\frac{1}{4}$ teaspoon salt
$3\frac{1}{2}$ cups flour
extra butter to grease the cookie sheets

DIRECTIONS:

1. Stir the butter and sugar together until well mixed.

2. Add the eggs, baking soda and salt.

3. Add the flour and mix thoroughly.

4. Place the dough on a large sheet of waxed paper and shape into a roll 2″ in diameter. Wrap the waxed paper around the roll of dough and allow to chill overnight in the refrigerator.

5. Next day, preheat the oven to 350°.

6. Cut the dough into $\frac{1}{8}$″ slices.

7. Grease the cookie sheets with the extra butter and then place the cookies on them about an inch apart.

8. Bake for 12 minutes. Makes about four dozen cookies.

Little Lemon Cookies

These soft lemony cookies have a wonderful flavor and are super-easy to make.

INGREDIENTS:

½ cup butter
3 tablespoons fresh lemon juice
1 cup sugar
1 egg, beaten
3 cups flour
¼ teaspoon baking soda
¼ cup sour cream
extra butter to grease the cookie sheets

DIRECTIONS:

1. Stir the butter, lemon juice and sugar together thoroughly.

2. Beat in the egg. Add the flour and baking soda.

3. Combine the flour mixture with the sour cream and mix well. The dough should have a soft consistency.

4. Place the dough on a large piece of waxed paper and shape into a roll two inches thick. Wrap the waxed paper around the roll of dough and allow to chill overnight in the refrigerator.

5. Next day, preheat the oven to 350°.

6. Now that the dough is firm cut it into $\frac{1}{8}''$ slices.

7. Grease the cookie sheets with the extra butter and then place the cookies on them about an inch apart.

8. Bake for ten minutes. Makes about four dozen cookies.

Chocolate Bar Cookies

This dough is spread on a cookie sheet, baked and then cut into bars.

INGREDIENTS:

$\frac{1}{4}$ cup butter
2 squares unsweetened chocolate (2 ounces)
$\frac{2}{3}$ cup sugar
1 cup finely chopped almonds
2 eggs
$\frac{1}{2}$ cup flour
extra butter to grease the cookie sheets
extra confectioner's sugar, sifted

DIRECTIONS:

1. Preheat the oven to 350°.

2. In a large saucepan, over medium heat, combine the butter, chocolate and sugar. Stir until they are completely melted.

3. Remove the mixture from the stove and add the almonds. Stir the mixture well again.

4. Mix in the eggs and the flour. With the extra butter grease the cookie sheet.

5. Spread the dough about half an inch thick on the cookie sheet. Bake for 15 minutes.

6. Allow to cool for 10 minutes and then cut into bars. Makes about thirty-five two-inch bar cookies.